Highlights

Hidden Pictures

On the Move
아슬아슬 탈 것

Super Challenge 숨은그림찾기

소란i

슈퍼 챌린지 숨은그림찾기에 도전하게 된 것을 환영합니다!

숨은그림찾기를 마치면 √ 표시를 하세요. 숨은그림찾기를 하며 즐거운 시간을 보내기 바랍니다.

차례

- ☐ 멋진 하프파이프 시범 Half-Pipe Exhibition — 4
- ☐ 돌고래 관찰 Dolphin Watching — 5
- ☐ 칙칙폭폭 산악 특급열차 Mountain Express — 6
- ☐ 시냇물에 종이배가 둥둥 Paper Boats — 7
- ☐ 노새의 휴일 Mule's Day Off — 8
- ☐ 쌩쌩, 활강 단거리 경기 Downhill Dash — 9
- ☐ 굉장한 롤러스케이트 경주 The Great Skate Race — 10
- ☐ 선상가옥 생활 Life on a Houseboat — 11
- ☐ 즐거운 가족 휴가여행 Family Vacation — 12
- ☐ 기우뚱거리는 카누에서 In a Tippy Canoe — 13
- ☐ 자, 간다! Here We Go! — 14
- ☐ 새 도로 건설 Building a New Road — 15
- ☐ 무동력 자동차 경주대회 Soapbox Racers — 16
- ☐ 안전한 항구로 Safe Harbor — 18
- ☐ 바깥나들이 Out and About — 19
- ☐ 새끼 에뮤들의 유모차 타기 Baby Emus' Buggy Ride — 20
- ☐ 눈의 여왕 The Snow Queen — 21
- ☐ 아슬아슬, 곡예 비행사 Barnstormer — 22
- ☐ 철도 공사 Working on the Railroad — 23
- ☐ 구조작업 To the Rescue — 24
- ☐ 피커딜리 광장 전 정류장 Next Stop: Piccadilly Circus — 25
- ☐ 동물 자전거 그룹 Animal Peloton — 26
- ☐ 아름다운 기구 타고 둥실 In a Beautiful Balloon — 28
- ☐ 신기한 외계인과의 만남 Alien Encounter — 29
- ☐ 제트스키 승리! The Jet Ski Wins — 30
- ☐ 터널을 지나며 내뿜는 증기 Steaming through the Tunnel — 31
- ☐ 다 함께 롤러스케이트를! Everybody, Skate! — 32
- ☐ 우주로 발사! Blast Off! — 34
- ☐ 신나는 빙상요트 레이스 Ice Sailing — 35
- ☐ 다리 건설자들 Bridge Builders — 36
- ☐ 샌프란시스코 거리 Streets of San Francisco — 38
- ☐ 항해하기 좋은 운동화 Seaworthy Sneaker — 39
- ☐ 잠시 휴식하기 Taking a Break — 40
- ☐ 아이고, 이런! Oops! — 41
- ☐ 덜커덩거리는 고물 자동차 Jumping Jalopy — 42
- ☐ 배를 끌고 가는 예인선 테드 Tugboat Ted — 43
- ☐ 대단한 탈출 A Great Escape — 44
- ☐ 자세 바꾸기 Switch Stance — 46
- ☐ 드르륵드르륵, 큰 바퀴 자전거 Big-Wheel Bikes — 47
- ☐ 흙 파는 기계들 Earth Movers — 48
- ☐ 두근두근, 이륙 준비 Ready for Takeoff — 50
- ☐ 즐거운 스케이트보드 데이트 Skate Date — 52
- ☐ 바람을 향하여 Into the Wind — 53
- ☐ 고양이들이 앞서다 The Cats Pull Ahead — 54
- ☐ 해변 즐기기 Surfside Fun — 56
- ☐ 쉭쉭, 비탈길 달리기 Downhill Run — 57
- ☐ 에디의 스쿠터 Eddie's Scooter — 58
- ☐ 아빠와 함께 선착장으로 Down at the Dock — 59
- ☐ 우주 탐험가 Space Explorer — 60
- ☐ 2인용 자전거 타기 Two for the Road — 61
- ☐ 도로변 작은 식당에서 At the Diner — 62
- ☐ 착륙 시작! Coming In for a Landing — 63
- ☐ 악어의 공중부양 Gator Gets Air — 64
- ☐ 구조 크레인 출동 Cherry Picker to the Rescue — 65
- ☐ 급류 타는 거북이들 Whitewater Turtles — 66
- ☐ 하늘을 나는 표범 Leopard in Flight — 67
- ☐ 해협 건너기 Across the Channel — 68
- ☐ 생쥐들의 도로경주 Rodent Road Race — 70

Cover Illustration by Charles Jordan

- ☐ 철도 건널목 Railroad Crossing ... 71
- ☐ 과연 날까? But Will It Fly? ... 72
- ☐ 와, 육지다! Land, Ho! ... 73
- ☐ 일요일 공원에서 Sunday in the Park ... 74
- ☐ 자동차 여행 중 On the Road ... 75
- ☐ 즐거운 트롤리 Jolly Trolley ... 76
- ☐ 소방선 훈련 Fireboat Drill ... 77
- ☐ 신나는 스키 학교 Ski School ... 78
- ☐ 강 위의 배에서 On the Riverboat ... 79
- ☐ 호수에서 At the Lake ... 80
- ☐ 스카이다이빙하는 스컹크들 Skydiving Skunks ... 81
- ☐ 경주 시작! They're Off! ... 82
- ☐ 신기한 무중력 Zero Gravity ... 83
- ☐ 강가의 친구들 Friends on the River ... 84
- ☐ 마지막 회전 The Last Turn ... 86
- ☐ 어이, 이봐! Ahoy There! ... 87
- ☐ 들어오세요 Coming Through ... 88
- ☐ 비행학교 Flight School ... 89
- ☐ 거친 급류타기 Wild Ride ... 90
- ☐ 가파른 비탈길 Steep Grade ... 91
- ☐ 에버글레이드 습지 여행 Touring the Everglades ... 92
- ☐ 자유를 즐기는 덩치 큰 사슴 Moose on the Loose ... 94
- ☐ 흥미진진한 우주 서핑 Space Surfing ... 95
- ☐ 강을 따라 떠내려가기 Floating Down the River ... 96
- ☐ 쥐 자전거 경주 Rat Race ... 98
- ☐ 통학버스 타기 Boarding the School Bus ... 99
- ☐ 수상스키 타는 펠리컨 Pelican on Waterskis ... 100
- ☐ 근사한 경관 비행 Scenic Flight ... 101
- ☐ 크로스컨트리 관찰하기 Cross-Country Sighting ... 102
- ☐ 높은 자전거 타고 룰루랄라 On a High-Wheeler ... 103
- ☐ 오스트레일리아 관광버스 Tour Bus Down Under ... 104
- ☐ 요트 레이스 Yacht Race ... 105
- ☐ 다리 위에 멈춘 고장 난 차 Breakdown on the Bridge ... 106
- ☐ 운하의 곤돌라들 Gondolas on the Canal ... 107
- ☐ 리프트 타고 정상으로 Lift to the Top ... 108
- ☐ 시험비행 Test Flight ... 109
- ☐ 누가 빨리 내려갈까 Race to the Bottom ... 110
- ☐ 반가운 귀항 Return from the Sea ... 112
- ☐ 장거리 자전거 여행 Long-Distance Ride ... 113
- ☐ 교외 드라이브 A Drive in the Country ... 114
- ☐ 어촌마을 Fisherman's Cove ... 115
- ☐ 자전거 탄 토끼 Bunny on a Bike ... 116
- ☐ 뭉게구름 배경의 요트들 Ahead of the Clouds ... 117
- ☐ 미끄러운 비탈길 즐기기 Slippery Slope ... 118
- ☐ 농약 살포 비행기 Crop Duster ... 119
- ☐ 중장비 작업장 Heavy Equipment ... 120
- ☐ 특별 구매 Special Purchase ... 122
- ☐ 즐거운 여행! Bon Voyage ... 124
- ☐ 비탈 아래로 프리라이딩 Freeriding Downhill ... 125
- ☐ 하늘을 수놓은 멋진 에어 쇼 Air Show ... 126
- ☐ 통나무 나르기 Loads of Logs ... 128
- ☐ 금문교를 지나 Through the Golden Gate ... 130
- ☐ 정답 Answers ... 131

멋진 하프파이프 시범 Half-Pipe Exhibition

초승달 crescent moon, 핸드벨 handbell, 빨대 drinking straw, 반지 ring, 골프채 golf club, 드라이버 screwdriver, 돋보기 magnifying glass, 물고기 fish, 페인트 붓 paintbrush, 버섯 mushroom, 나무망치 mallet, 모자 hat, 하트 heart, 숟가락 spoon, 삼각기 pennant, 사다리 ladder, 양초 candle, 찻잔 teacup, 컵케이크 cupcake, 연필 pencil, 깔때기 funnel, 핀셋 tweezers, 바늘 needle

돌고래 관찰 Dolphin Watching

막대 아이스크림 ice-cream bar, 프라이팬 frying pan, 장갑 glove, 반지 ring, 찻주전자 teapot, 열쇠 key, 달걀 egg, 파리채 flyswatter, 망원경 telescope, 칫솔 toothbrush, 잠자리 dragonfly, 앵무새 parrot, 토끼 rabbit

Illustrated by Valeri Gorbachev

칙칙폭폭, 산악 특급열차 Mountain Express

옥수수 ear of corn, 선인장 cactus, 야구모자 baseball cap, 지팡이 모양 사탕 candy cane, 카메라 camera, 찻잔 teacup, 빗 comb, 컵케이크 cupcake, 당근 carrot, 사탕 piece of candy, 애벌레 caterpillar, 페인트 통 can of paint

시냇물에 종이배가 둥둥 Paper Boats

야구 방망이 baseball bat, 핸드벨 handbell, 칫솔 toothbrush, 양초 candle, 카누 canoe, 셀러리 celery, 찻잔 teacup, 컵케이크 cupcake, 물고기 fish, 손전등 flashlight, 모자 hat, 음표 musical note, 파이 조각 slice of pie, 백조 swan, 꽃삽 trowel

도전! 슈퍼 챌린지!
14개의 숨은그림을 찾아라!

노새의 휴일
Mule's Day Off

쌩쌩, 활강 단거리 경기 Downhill Dash

파이 조각 slice of pie, 종 bell, 아이스크림콘 ice-cream cone, 칫솔 toothbrush, 케이크 조각 slice of cake, 세탁용 솔 scrub brush, 연필 pencil, 푸시핀 pushpin, 크레용 crayon, 그림 붓 artist's brush, 낚싯바늘 fishhook, 도토리 acorn

굉장한 롤러스케이트 경주 The Great Skate Race

압정 tack, 소화전 fire hydrant, 종 bell, 빨래집게 clothespin, 초승달 crescent moon, 별 star, 도끼 ax, 편자(말발굽에 붙이는 쇳조각) horseshoe, 버섯 mushroom, 백열전구 light bulb, 찻잔 teacup, 등(스텐드) lamp, 잠자리 dragonfly

선상가옥 생활 Life on a Houseboat

활 archer's bow, 야구모자 baseball cap, 장갑 glove, 머그잔 mug, 파이 pie, 펴놓은 책 open book, 그릇 bowl, 크레용 crayon, 모자 hat, 백열전구 light bulb, 곡괭이 pickax, 뱀 snake

즐거운 가족 휴가여행 Family Vacation

하트 heart, 개 dog, 물개 seal, 별 star, 자 ruler, 장갑 glove, 시계 clock, 돛단배 sailboat, 안경 eyeglasses, 칫솔 toothbrush, 톱 saw, 돋보기 magnifying glass, 찻잔 teacup, 양말 sock

Illustrated by Tim Davis

기우뚱거리는 카누에서 In a Tippy Canoe

오리 duck, 접은 우산 closed umbrella, 백열전구 light bulb, 컵 cup, 나무망치 mallet, 낚싯바늘 fishhook, 반지 ring, 칫솔 toothbrush, 연필 pencil, 양동이 pail, 플런저(흡인식 하수관 청소기) plunger, 포크 fork, 펭귄 penguin

Illustrated by Valeri Gorbachev

자, 간다! Here We Go!

부메랑 boomerang, 옷걸이 coat hanger, 초승달 crescent moon, 망치 hammer, 하트 두 개 2 hearts, 열쇠 key, 장갑 glove, 박쥐 bat, 나비 butterfly, 빗 comb, 낚싯바늘 fishhook, 하이힐 구두 high-heeled shoe, 백열전구 light bulb, 곡괭이 pickax, 양말 sock

Illustrated by Arieh Zeldich

새 도로 건설 Building a New Road

펜 pen, 그림 붓 artist's brush, 골프채 golf club, 크레용 crayon, 칫솔 toothbrush, 호루라기 whistle, 나무망치 mallet, 숟가락 spoon, 열쇠 key, 돋보기 magnifying glass, 벙어리장갑 mitten, 신발 shoe

Illustrated by Charles Jordan

15

무동력 자동차 경주대회
Soapbox Racers

*Soapbox: 직접 만든 경주용 차

도전! 슈퍼 챌린지! 24개의 숨은그림을 찾아라!

안전한 항구로 Safe Harbor

깃발 flag, 초승달 crescent moon, 펜 pen, 편자(말발굽에 붙이는 쇳조각) horseshoe, 낚싯바늘 fishhook, 사다리 ladder, 하키 스틱 hockey stick, 쇠스랑 pitchfork, 못 nail, 빗 comb, 도미노 패 domino, 곡괭이 pickax, 돌고래 dolphin, 실패 spool of thread, 옷걸이 coat hanger, 야구 방망이 baseball bat, 신발 shoe, 단추 button

Illustrated by Arieh Zeldich

바깥나들이 Out and About

양초 candle, 장갑 glove, 롤러스케이트 roller skate, 망치 hammer, 연필 pencil, 케이크 조각 slice of cake, 남성 정장용 모자 top hat, 돛단배 sailboat, 토끼 rabbit, 펴놓은 책 open book, 톱 saw, 찻주전자 teapot, 버터나이프 butter knife

새끼 에뮤들의 유모차 타기 Baby Emus' Buggy Ride

토끼 rabbit, 당근 carrot, 개구리 frog, 물고기 fish, 백열전구 light bulb, 양초 candle, 돋보기 magnifying glass, 부메랑 boomerang, 빗 comb, 도마뱀 lizard, 닻 anchor, 쥐 mouse, 물 주전자 pitcher, 손전등 flashlight

*에뮤: 날지 못하는 오스트레일리아산 큰 새

Illustrated by Valeri Gorbachev

눈의 여왕 The Snow Queen

지팡이 cane, 플런저(흡인식 하수관 청소기) plunger, 접은 우산 closed umbrella, 막대 아이스크림 ice-cream bar, 아이스크림콘 ice-cream cone, 종 bell, 열쇠 key, 오렌지 조각 slice of orange, 반지 ring, 왕관 crown, 도미노 패 domino, 실패 spool of thread, 낚싯바늘 fishhook

Illustrated by Arieh Zeldich

아슬아슬, 곡예 비행사 Barnstormer

신발 shoe, 종 bell, 괭이 hoe, 안전핀 safety pin, 푸시핀 pushpin, 사과 반쪽 apple half, 벙어리장갑 mitten, 컵케이크 cupcake, 책 book, 빗 comb, 깃털 feather, 꽃삽 trowel, 페인트 붓 paintbrush, 무 radish, 연필 pencil, 펜치 pliers

Illustrated by Charles Jordan

철도 공사 Working on the Railroad

책 세 권 3 books, 부츠 boot, 그릇 bowl, 닭 chicken, 초승달 crescent moon, 안경 eyeglasses, 손전등 flashlight, 잔(손잡이가 없고 굽이 달린) goblet, 망치 hammer, 편자(말발굽에 붙이는 쇳조각) horseshoe, 못 nail, 숟가락 spoon

Illustrated by Kit Wray

구조작업
To the Rescue

도전! 슈퍼 챌린지!
14개의 숨은그림을 찾아라!

피커딜리 광장 전 정류장 Next Stop: Piccadilly Circus

손목시계 wristwatch, 그림 붓 artist's brush, 망치 hammer, 하이힐 부츠 high-heeled boot, 종 bell, 하키 스틱 hockey stick, 안전핀 safety pin, 별 star, 새 bird, 여행 가방 suitcase, 망원경 telescope, 선물 present, 나침판 compass, 깃털 feather, 모자 hat, 카누 canoe

Illustrated by Jeri Simkus

동물 자전거 그룹 Animal Peloton

사과 심 apple core, 화살 arrow, 핸드벨 handbell, 부츠 boot, 빗자루 broom, 빨래집게 clothespin, 빗 comb, 오리 duck, 쓰레받기 dustpan, 포크 fork, 망치 hammer, 아이스크림콘 ice-cream cone, 곤충 insect, 다리미 iron, 쥐 mouse, 클립 paper clip, 연필 pencil, 롤러스케이트 roller skate, 돛단배 sailboat, 톱 saw, 상어 shark, 삽 shovel, 숟가락 spoon, 여행 가방 suitcase, 곰 인형 teddy bear, 전화 수화기 telephone receiver, 치약 튜브 tube of toothpaste, 새 bird, 거북이 turtle

Illustrated by Valeri Gorbachev

아름다운 기구 타고 둥실! In a Beautiful Balloon

토끼 rabbit, 피리 flute, 원숭이 monkey, 새 bird, 양동이 bucket, 꽃 flower, 팽이 toy top, 우산 umbrella, 부츠 boot, 돛단배 sailboat, 펴놓은 책 open book, 수탉의 머리 rooster's head, H글자 letter H

Illustrated by Jeri Simkus

신기한 외계인과의 만남 Alien Encounter

막대 아이스크림 ice pop, 아이스크림소다수 ice-cream soda, 못 nail, 반지 ring, 망치 hammer, 압정 tack, 오리 duck, 파이 조각 slice of pie, 백열전구 light bulb, 손목시계 wristwatch, 신발 shoe, 고래 whale, 컵케이크 cupcake

제트스키 승리! The Jet Ski Wins

반지 ring, 도미노 패 domino, 골프채 golf club, 신호기 pennant, 낚싯바늘 fishhook, 옷걸이 coat hanger, 하트 두 개 2 hearts, 하키 스틱 hockey stick, 부메랑 boomerang, 열쇠 key, 럭비공 football, 플런저(흡인식 하수관 청소기) plunger, 카메라 camera, 백열전구 light bulb, 사다리 ladder

Illustrated by Arieh Zeldich

터널을 지나며 내뿜는 증기 Steaming through the Tunnel

책 book, 안경 eyeglasses, 칫솔 toothbrush, 닭의 머리 chicken's head, 모자 hat, 건전지 battery, 나무망치 mallet, 하트 heart, 가위 scissors, 목걸이 necklace, 박쥐 bat, 클립 paper clip, 장갑 glove, 비행기 airplane

Illustrated by Tim Davis

다 함께 롤러스케이트를!
Everybody, Skate!

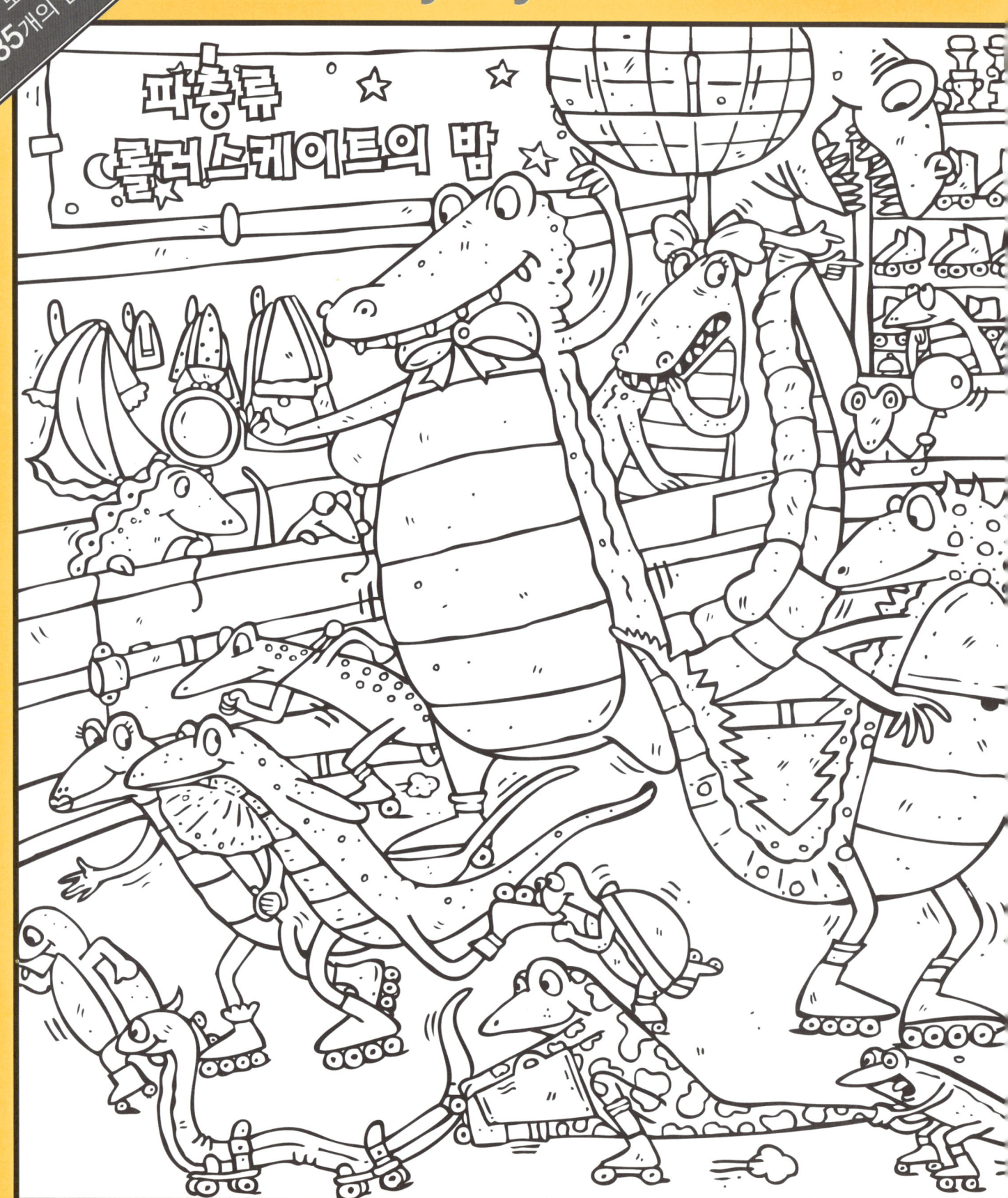

우주로 발사! Blast Off!

야구 방망이 baseball bat, 핸드벨 handbell, 신호기 pennant, 포크 fork, 하트 heart, 아이스크림콘 ice-cream cone, 열쇠 key, 칼 knife, 못 nail, 바늘 needle, 반지 ring, 신발 shoe, 뱀 snake, 칫솔 toothbrush, v자형 뼈(위시본) wishbone, 벌레 worm

Illustrated by R. Michael Palan

신나는 빙상요트 레이스 Ice Sailing

코바늘 crochet hook, 야구 방망이 baseball bat, 케이크 조각 slice of cake, 하트 heart, 못 nail, 벙어리장갑 mitten, 버섯 mushroom, 안전핀 safety pin, 신호기 pennant, 버터나이프 butter knife, 노 paddle, 연필 pencil, 골프채 golf club, 당근 carrot

다리 건설자들 Bridge Builders

양말 sock, 빗 comb, 펴놓은 책 open book, 편지봉투 envelope, 부메랑 boomerang, 골프채 golf club, 페인트 붓 paintbrush, 톱 saw, 물고기 fish, 압정 tack, 실패 spool of thread, 연필 pencil

샌프란시스코 거리 Streets of San Francisco

사다리 ladder, 새 bird, 자 ruler, 찻잔 teacup, 신발 shoe, 망원경 telescope, 골프채 golf club, 여자의 머리 woman's head, 안경 eyeglasses, 돛단배 sailboat, 말의 머리 horse's head, 그림 붓 artist's brush, 연필 pencil, 바구니 속 돼지 piglet in a basket, 요정의 모자 elf's hat

항해하기 좋은 운동화 Seaworthy Sneaker

전화 수화기 telephone receiver, 다리미 iron, 잠자리 dragonfly, 톱 saw, 나비 리본 bow, 숟가락 spoon, 신호기 pennant, 머그잔 mug, 하이힐 구두 high-heeled shoe, 병아리 chick, 열쇠 key, 요정의 모자 elf's hat, 애벌레 caterpillar, 클립 paper clip

잠시 휴식하기 Taking a Break

그림 붓 artist's brush, 나무망치 mallet, 음표 musical note, 연필 pencil, 크레용 crayon, 책 book, 왕관 crown, 돋보기 magnifying glass, 괭이 hoe, 골프채 golf club, 안경 eyeglasses, 손전등 flashlight

아이고, 이런! Oops!

천막 tepee, 버섯 mushroom, 찻잔 teacup, 꽃 flower, 하트 heart, 종 bell, 뱀 snake, V자형 뼈(위시본) wishbone, 바늘 needle, 자 ruler, 요-요 yo-yo, 올리브 olive, 숟가락 spoon, 반지 ring

덜커덩거리는 고물 자동차 Jumping Jalopy

부메랑 boomerang, 코끼리의 머리 elephant's head, 새 bird, 하트 heart, 아이스크림콘 ice-cream cone, 딸기 strawberry, 돋보기 magnifying glass, 달팽이 snail, 곡괭이 pickax, 모자 hat, 물고기 fish, 칫솔 toothbrush, 열쇠 key, 바지 pair of pants, 반지 ring

배를 끌고 가는 예인선 테드 Tugboat Ted

사과 apple, 도끼 ax, 풍선 balloon, 새 bird, 하트 heart, 대걸레 mop, 버섯 mushroom, 연필 pencil, 파이 조각 slice of pie, 드라이버 screwdriver, 뱀 snake, 팽이 toy top, 수박 watermelon

Illustrated by George Wildman

43

대단한 탈출 A Great Escape

열쇠 key, 뱀 snake, 반지 ring, 아이스크림콘 ice-cream cone, 빵 조각 slice of bread, 숟가락 spoon, 빨대 drinking straw, 파이 조각 slice of pie, 빗 comb, 양초 candle, 카누 canoe, v자형 뼈(위시본) wishbone, 찻잔 teacup, 장갑 glove, 못 nail, 머리빗 hairbrush, 막대사탕 lollipop, 병 bottle, 편지 letter, 물고기 fish, 칫솔 toothbrush, 포크 fork, 악어 alligator, 톱 saw

Illustrated by Ron Lieser

45

자세 바꾸기
Switch Stance

도전! 슈퍼 챌린지!
16개의 숨은그림을 찾아라!

드르륵드르륵, 큰 바퀴 자전거 Big-Wheel Bikes

바나나 banana, 종 bell, 부츠 boot, 깃털 feather, 물고기 fish, 포크 fork, 개구리 frog, 장갑 glove, 나방 moth, 파이 조각 slice of pie, 반지 ring, 숟가락 spoon, 거북이 turtle

흙 파는 기계들 Earth Movers

자 ruler, 드릴 drill, 도시락통 lunchbox, 나무망치 mallet, 못 nail, 드라이버 screwdriver, 연필 pencil, 삽 shovel, 톱 saw, 나사 screw, 부츠 boot, 꽃삽 trowel

두근두근, 이륙 준비 Ready for Takeoff

괭이 hoe, 삽 shovel, 프라이팬 frying pan, 푸시핀 pushpin, 골프채 golf club, 머그잔 mug, 펜 pen, 종 bell, 깃털 feather, 나무망치 mallet, 그림 붓 artist's brush, 못 nail, 신발 shoe, 연필 pencil, 아이스크림콘 ice-cream cone, 머리빗 hairbrush, 파이 조각 slice of pie, 크레용 crayon, 버섯 mushroom, 부침용 주걱 spatula, 열쇠 key, 양초 candle, 음표 musical note, 케이크 조각 slice of cake

즐거운 스케이트보드 데이트
Skate Date

도전! 슈퍼 챌린지!
13개의 숨은그림을 찾아라!

바람을 향하여 Into the Wind

숟가락 spoon, 깃털 feather, 달팽이 snail, 개구리 frog, 빗자루 broom, 백조 swan, 편지봉투 envelope, 빗 comb, 야구모자 baseball cap, 큰 부리 새의 머리 toucan's head, 새 bird, 삼각기 pennant, 크레용 crayon, 연 kite

Illustrated by Kit Wray

53

고양이들이 앞서다 The Cats Pull Ahead

부침용 주걱 spatula, 깃털 feather, 괭이 hoe, 연필 pencil, 쓰레받기 dustpan, 벙어리장갑 mitten, 반지 ring, 깃발 flag, 당근 carrot, 피자 조각 slice of pizza, 머리빗 hairbrush, 바나나 banana, 케이크 조각 slice of cake, 머그잔 mug, 돛단배 sailboat, 양초 candle, 못 nail, 안전핀 safety pin, 그림 붓 artist's brush, 푸시핀 pushpin, 치약 튜브 tube of toothpaste, 파이 조각 slice of pie, 핸드백 handbag, 양말 sock, 책 book, 골프채 golf club, 자전거 공기 주입기 bicycle pump

Illustrated by Charles Jordan

해변 즐기기
Surfside Fun

도전! 슈퍼 챌린지!
12개의 숨은그림을 찾아라!

쉭쉭, 비탈길 달리기 Downhill Run

찻잔 teacup, 골프채 golf club, 아이스크림콘 ice-cream cone, 그림 붓 artist's brush, 못 nail, 펜 pen, 디저트 접시 dessert dish, 종 bell, 책 book, 연필 pencil, 반지 ring, 케이크 조각 slice of cake

Illustrated by Charles Jordan

에디의 스쿠터 Eddie's Scooter

칫솔 toothbrush, 펜 pen, 파이 조각 slice of pie, 열쇠 key, 깔때기 funnel, 페인트 붓 paintbrush, 찻잔 teacup, 연필 pencil, 사과 조각 wedge of apple, 국자 ladle, 신발 shoe, 압정 tack

Illustrated by Charles Jordan

아빠와 함께 선착장으로 Down at the Dock

v자형 뼈(위시본) wishbone, 커피포트 coffeepot, 칫솔 toothbrush, 다리미 iron, 냄비 saucepan, 드라이버 screwdriver, 페인트 붓 paintbrush, 크레용 crayon, 당근 carrot, 양말 sock, 편지봉투 envelope, 파이 조각 slice of pie, 안전핀 safety pin

Illustrated by Leslie Franz

우주 탐험가 Space Explorer

바나나 banana, 종 bell, 돛단배 sailboat, 백열전구 light bulb, 양초 candle, 왕관 crown, 찻잔 teacup, 물고기 fish, 개구리 frog, 하트 heart, 아이스크림콘 ice-cream cone, 반지 ring, 톱 saw, 숟가락 spoon, 칫솔 toothbrush

2인용 자전거 타기 Two for the Road

개 dog, 달 moon, 연필 pencil, 찻잔 teacup, 숟가락 spoon, 부츠 boot, 드라이버 screwdriver, 망치 hammer, 벙어리장갑 mitten, 뱀 snake, 바늘 needle, 칫솔 toothbrush

도로변 작은 식당에서 At the Diner

손도끼hatchet, 피자 조각slice of pizza, 바늘needle, 요정의 모자elf's hat, 반지ring, 연필pencil, 남성 정장용 모자top hat, 사과apple, 삼각기pennant, 팝콘 주머니bag of popcorn, 초승달crescent moon, 찻잔teacup, 골프채golf club, 케이크 조각slice of cake, 바나나banana, 빨대drinking straw, 아이스크림콘ice-cream cone

착륙 시작! Coming In for a Landing

양초 candle, 책 book, 막대 아이스크림 ice-cream bar, 삼각기 pennant, 반지 ring, 케이크 조각 slice of cake, 자전거 공기 주입기 bicycle pump, 무 turnip, 낚싯바늘 fishhook, 푸시핀 pushpin, 냄비 saucepan, 압정 tack

Illustrated by Charles Jordan

63

악어의 공중부양
Gator Gets Air

도전! 슈퍼 챌린지!
15개의 숨은그림을 찾아라!

구조 크레인 출동 Cherry Picker to the Rescue

나무망치 mallet, v자형 뼈(위시본) wishbone, 깔때기 funnel, 책 book, 반지 ring, 양초 candle, 버섯 mushroom, 드라이버 screwdriver, 당근 carrot, 안전핀 safety pin, 낚싯바늘 fishhook, 아이스크림콘 ice-cream cone

급류 타는 거북이들 Whitewater Turtles

찻잔 teacup, 숟가락 spoon, 편지 letter, 초승달 crescent moon, 음표 musical note, 낚싯바늘 fishhook, 벙어리장갑 mitten, 사과 apple, 하이힐 구두 high-heeled shoe, 오리 duck, 바늘 needle, 못 nail, 그림 붓 artist's brush, 버섯 mushroom, v자형 뼈(위시본) wishbone, 크레용 crayon, 포크 fork, 왕관 crown

Illustrated by Mike DeSantis

하늘을 나는 표범 Leopard in Flight

나사 screw, 빗 comb, 황새 stork, 낚싯바늘 fishhook, 문어 octopus, 숟가락 spoon, 나비 리본 bow, 하트 heart, 아이스크림콘 ice-cream cone, 카우보이모자 cowboy hat, 파티 모자 party hat, 핸드벨 handbell, 인라인스케이트 inline skate

Illustrated by Valeri Gorbachev

해협 건너기
Across the Channel

생쥐들의 도로경주 Rodent Road Race

닭 chicken, 가위 scissors, 나팔 horn, 올빼미 owl, 백열전구 light bulb, 머리빗 hairbrush, 자물쇠 padlock, 핸드벨 handbell, 화살 arrow, 당근 carrot, 호박 pumpkin, 고양이 cat, 새 bird, 꽃병 vase

Illustrated by Valeri Gorbachev

철도 건널목 Railroad Crossing

양말 sock, 코끼리의 머리 elephant's head, 그림 붓 artist's brush, 밀방망이(반죽을 미는 데 쓰는) rolling pin, 찻주전자 teapot, 기름 치는 기구(기다란 주둥이가 달린) oil can, 왕의 머리 king's head, 아이스크림콘 ice-cream cone, 물고기 fish, 당근 carrot, 못 nail, 포크 fork, 개의 머리 dog's head, 가위 scissors, 연 kite, 칫솔 toothbrush, 그릇 bowl

Illustrated by Ralph Owen

71

과연 날까? But Will It Fly?

달걀 egg, 그릇 bowl, 깃발 flag, 책 book, 허리띠 belt, 백열전구 light bulb, 대걸레 mop, 도넛 doughnut, 잔(손잡이가 없고 굽이 달린) goblet, 못 nail, 압정 tack, 찻잔 teacup, 야구공 baseball, 곤충 insect

와, 육지다! Land, Ho!

박쥐 bat, 왕관 crown, 빗 comb, 망치 hammer, 하트 heart, 아이스크림콘 ice-cream cone, 쥐 mouse, 못 nail, 펴놓은 책 open book, 연필 pencil, 톱 saw, 상어 shark, 찻잔 teacup, 칫솔 toothbrush

일요일 공원에서 Sunday in the Park

사과 심 apple core, 당근 carrot, 케이크 조각 slice of cake, 요요 yo-yo, 종 bell, 마술봉 magic wand, 열쇠 key, 양초 candle, 못 nail, 푸시핀 pushpin, 버섯 mushroom, 안전핀 safety pin, 파이 조각 slice of pie

자동차 여행 중 On the Road

칫솔 toothbrush, 토끼 rabbit, 피자 pizza, 족제비 weasel, 연필 pencil, 책 book, 햄스터의 머리 hamster's head, 초승달 crescent moon, 숟가락 spoon, 홍관조의 머리 cardinal's head, 핫도그 hot dog, 쥐 mouse

Illustrated by Kit Wray

즐거운 트롤리 Jolly Trolley

젖병 baby's bottle, 부메랑 boomerang, 양초 candle, 초승달 crescent moon, 안경 eyeglasses, 골프채 golf club, 피자 pizza, 책 book, 나비 butterfly, 네 잎 클로버 four-leaf clover, 달걀 프라이 fried egg, 낚싯대 fishing pole, 하모니카 harmonica, 숟가락 spoon

소방선 훈련 Fireboat Drill

도미노 패 domino, 사다리 ladder, 안전핀 safety pin, 옷걸이 coat hanger, 클립 paper clip, 삽 shovel, 낚싯바늘 fishhook, 부메랑 boomerang, 푸시핀 pushpin, 노 paddle, 반지 ring, 하키 스틱 hockey stick, 오렌지 조각 slice of orange, 단추 button, 막대 아이스크림 ice-cream bar, 테니스공 tennis ball, 안경 eyeglasses

Illustrated by Arieh Zeldich

신나는 스키 학교 Ski School

새 birds, 찻잔 teacup, 옷걸이 coat hanger, 쥐 mouse, 클립 paper clip, 인라인스케이트 inline skate, 숟가락 spoon, 개미 ant, 솔 brush, 신호기 pennant, 바늘 needle, 연필 pencil, 거북이 turtle, 아이스크림콘 ice-cream cone

Illustrated by Valeri Gorbachev

강 위의 배에서 On the Riverboat

실패 spool of thread, 치즈 조각 wedge of cheese, 병 bottle, 개 dog, 톱 saw, 빗 comb, 오렌지 조각 slice of orange, 사다리 ladder, 새 bird, 밴조(악기) banjo, 칫솔 toothbrush, 물고기 fish, 요리 냄비 cooking pot

Illustrated by Georgina Hargreaves

79

호수에서 At the Lake

화살 arrow, 도마뱀 lizard, 빗자루 broom, 찻주전자 teapot, 활 archer's bow, 지팡이 cane, 호루라기 whistle, 연 kite, 펭귄 penguin, 물고기 fish, 새 bird, 개 dog, 클립 paper clip

스카이다이빙하는 스컹크들 Skydiving Skunks

괭이 hoe, 바늘 needle, 책 book, 깔때기 funnel, 편지봉투 envelope, 버섯 mushroom, 번개 lightning bolt, 종 bell, 럭비공 football, 반지 ring, 물고기 fish, 톱 saw, 땅콩 peanut, 칫솔 toothbrush

경주 시작!
They're Off!

도전! 슈퍼 챌린지!
13개의 숨은그림을 찾아라!

신기한 무중력 Zero Gravity

망원경 telescope, 렌치 wrench, 슬리퍼 slipper, 편지봉투 envelope, 칫솔 두 개 2 toothbrushes, 반지 ring, 백열전구 light bulb, 종 bell, 모자 hat, 실패 spool of thread, 막대 아이스크림 ice-cream bar, 찻잔 teacup, 핫도그 hot dog, 가위 scissors

강가의 친구들 Friends on the River

운동화 sneaker, 바나나 banana, 손전등 flashlight, 장갑 glove, 막대사탕 lollipop, 양초 candle, 깔때기 funnel, 찻잔 teacup, 프라이팬 frying pan, 빗자루 broom, 숟가락 spoon, 깃발 flag

마지막 회전 The Last Turn

바나나 banana, 왕관 crown, 안경 eyeglasses, 물고기 fish, 핸드벨 handbell, 모자 hat, 아이스크림콘 ice-cream cone, 연 kite, 클립 paper clip, 반지 ring, 뱀 snake, 침핀 straight pin, 칫솔 toothbrush

어이, 이봐!
Ahoy There!

도전! 슈퍼 챌린지!
12개의 숨은그림을 찾아라!

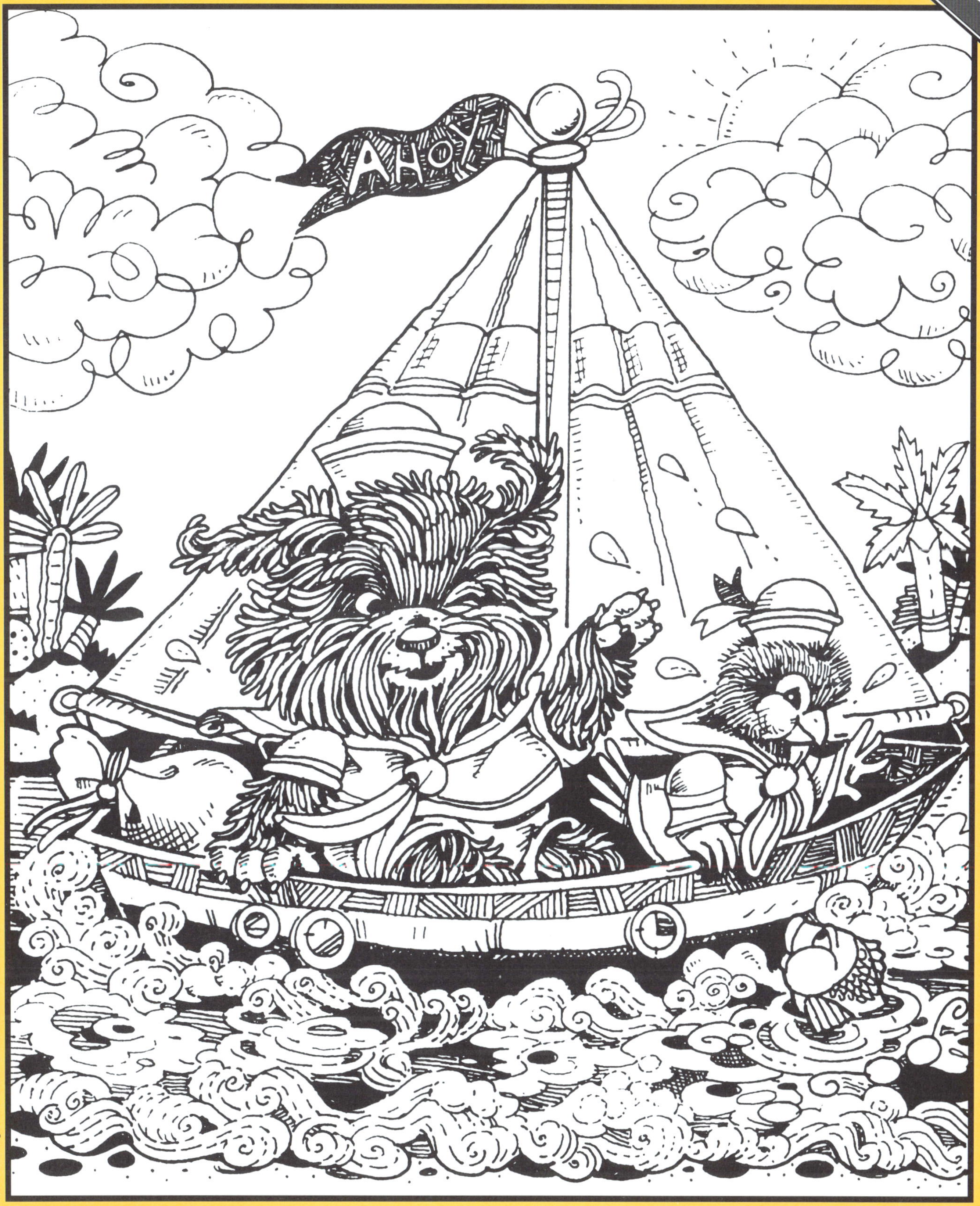

들어오세요 Coming Through

파이 조각 slice of pie, 깃발 flag, 바늘 needle, 펴놓은 책 open book, 뱀 snake, 막대사탕 lollipop, 종 bell, 양초 candle, 칫솔 toothbrush, 초승달 crescent moon, 기름통 oil drum, 사다리 ladder, 개 밥그릇 dog bowl

Illustrated by George Wildman

비행학교
Flight School

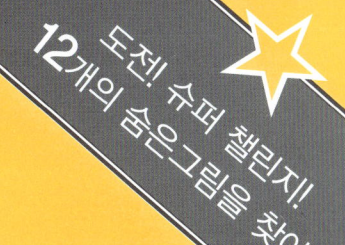
도전! 슈퍼 챌린지!
12개의 숨은그림을 찾아라!

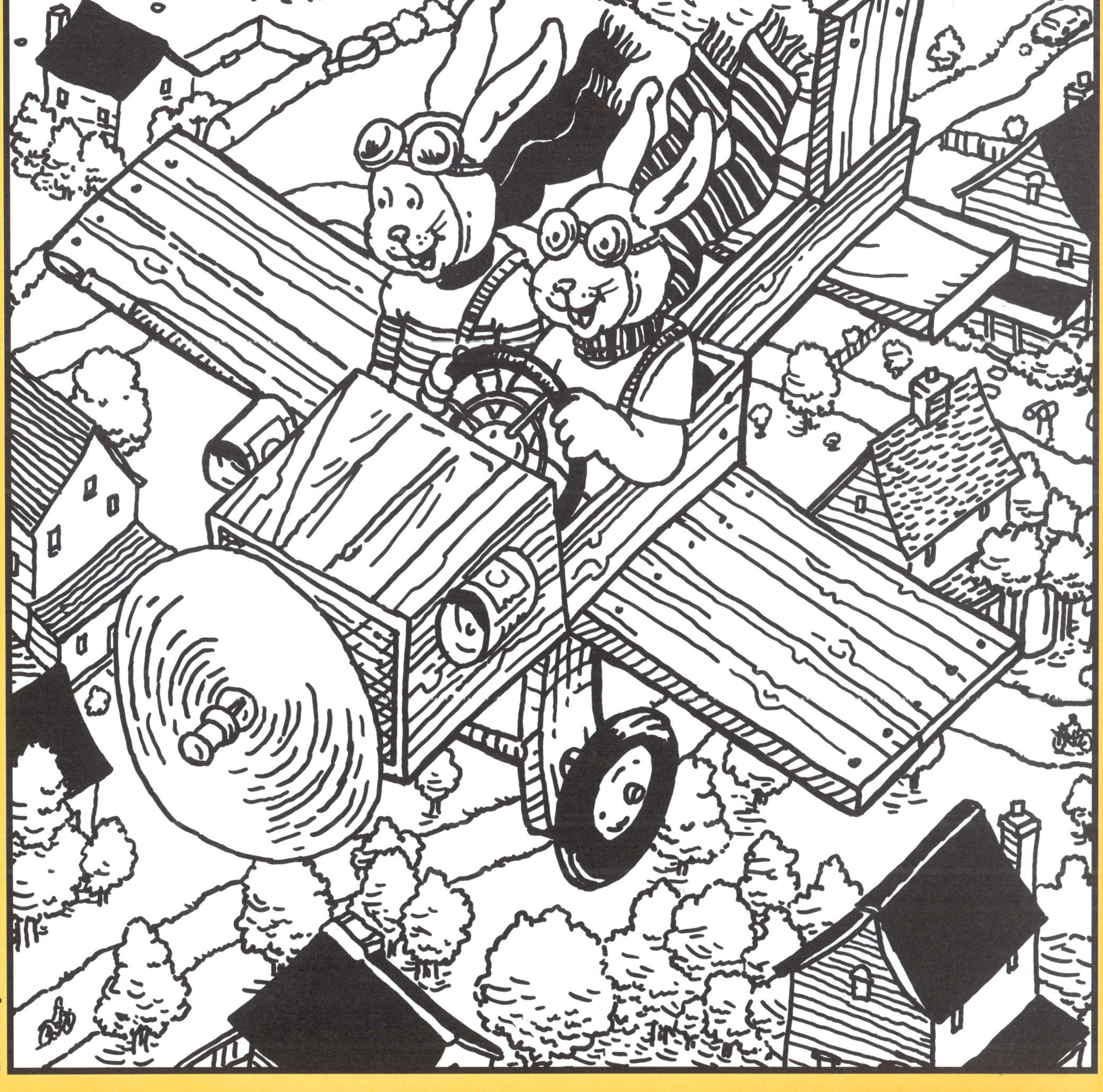

거친 급류타기 Wild Ride

포크 fork, 물고기 fish, 새 bird, 숟가락 spoon, 하트 heart, 초승달 crescent moon, 오리 duck, 못 nail, 손도끼 hatchet, 빗 comb, 뱀 snake, 쥐 mouse, 요정의 모자 elf's hat

가파른 비탈길 Steep Grade

아이스크림콘 ice-cream cone, 부침용 주걱 spatula, 나무망치 mallet, 실패 spool of thread, 종 bell, 깃털 feather, 펜 pen, 연필 pencil, 바나나 banana, 케이크 조각 slice of cake, 안전핀 safety pin, 버섯 mushroom

Illustrated by Charles Jordan

에버글레이드 습지 여행
Touring the Everglades

도전! 슈퍼 챌린지!
29개의 숨은그림을 찾아라!

자유를 즐기는 덩치 큰 사슴 Moose on the Loose

화살 arrow, 핸드벨 handbell, 새 bird, 개 dog, 오리 duck, 포크 fork, 머리빗 hairbrush, 다리미 iron, 열쇠 key, 숟가락 spoon, 못 nail, 신호기 pennant, 신발 shoe, 찻잔 teacup

Illustrated by Valeri Gorbachev

흥미진진한 우주 서핑 Space Surfing

바나나 banana, 선인장 cactus, 물고기 fish, 손전등 flashlight, 유령 ghost, 국자 ladle, 초승달 crescent moon, 바늘 needle, 반지 ring, 양말 sock, 꽃삽 trowel, 치약 튜브 tube of toothpaste, v자형 뼈(위시본) wishbone, 벌레 worm

Illustrated by R. Michael Palan

강을 따라 떠내려가기 Floating Down the River

달걀 프라이 fried egg, 지팡이 모양 사탕 candy cane, 핸드백 handbag, 펭귄 penguin, 삼각기 pennant, 바나나 banana, 새끼 물개 baby seal, 박쥐 bat, 하트 heart, 연필 pencil, 호박 pumpkin, 손전등 flashlight

쥐 자전거 경주 Rat Race

수박 조각 slice of watermelon, 지팡이 모양 사탕 candy cane, 화살 arrow, 낚싯바늘 fishhook, 햄버거 hamburger, 실패 spool of thread, 바늘 needle, 연필 pencil, 양초 candle, 삼각기 pennant, 압정 tack, 파이 조각 slice of pie, 유리컵 drinking glass, 망원경 telescope

Illustrated by Rocky Fuller

통학버스 타기 Boarding the School Bus

깃털 feather, 셀러리 celery, 파이 조각 slice of pie, 푸시핀 pushpin, 무 radish, 아이스크림콘 ice-cream cone, 자전거 공기 주입기 bicycle pump, 사다리 ladder, 케이크 조각 slice of cake, 반지 ring, 칫솔 toothbrush, 골프채 golf club

Illustrated by Charles Jordan

99

수상스키 타는 펠리컨 Pelican on Waterskis

부츠 boot, 초승달 crescent moon, 낚싯바늘 fishhook, 골프채 golf club, 손도끼 hatchet, 하트 heart, 고슴도치 hedgehog, 침핀 straight pin, 펴놓은 책 open book, 굴껍질 oyster shell, 파인애플 pineapple, 반지 ring, 가위 scissors

Illustrated by Arieh Zeldich

근사한 경관 비행 Scenic Flight

삽 shovel, 오리 duck, 머그잔 mug, 부츠 boot, 토끼 rabbit, 돛단배 sailboat, 초승달 crescent moon, 바늘 needle, 벌레 worm, 핀셋 tweezers, 벙어리장갑 mitten, 막대사탕 lollipop

크로스컨트리 관찰하기
Cross-Country Sighting

높은 자전거 타고 룰룰랄라
On a High-Wheeler

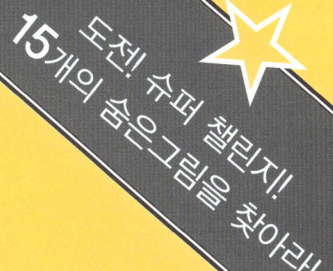

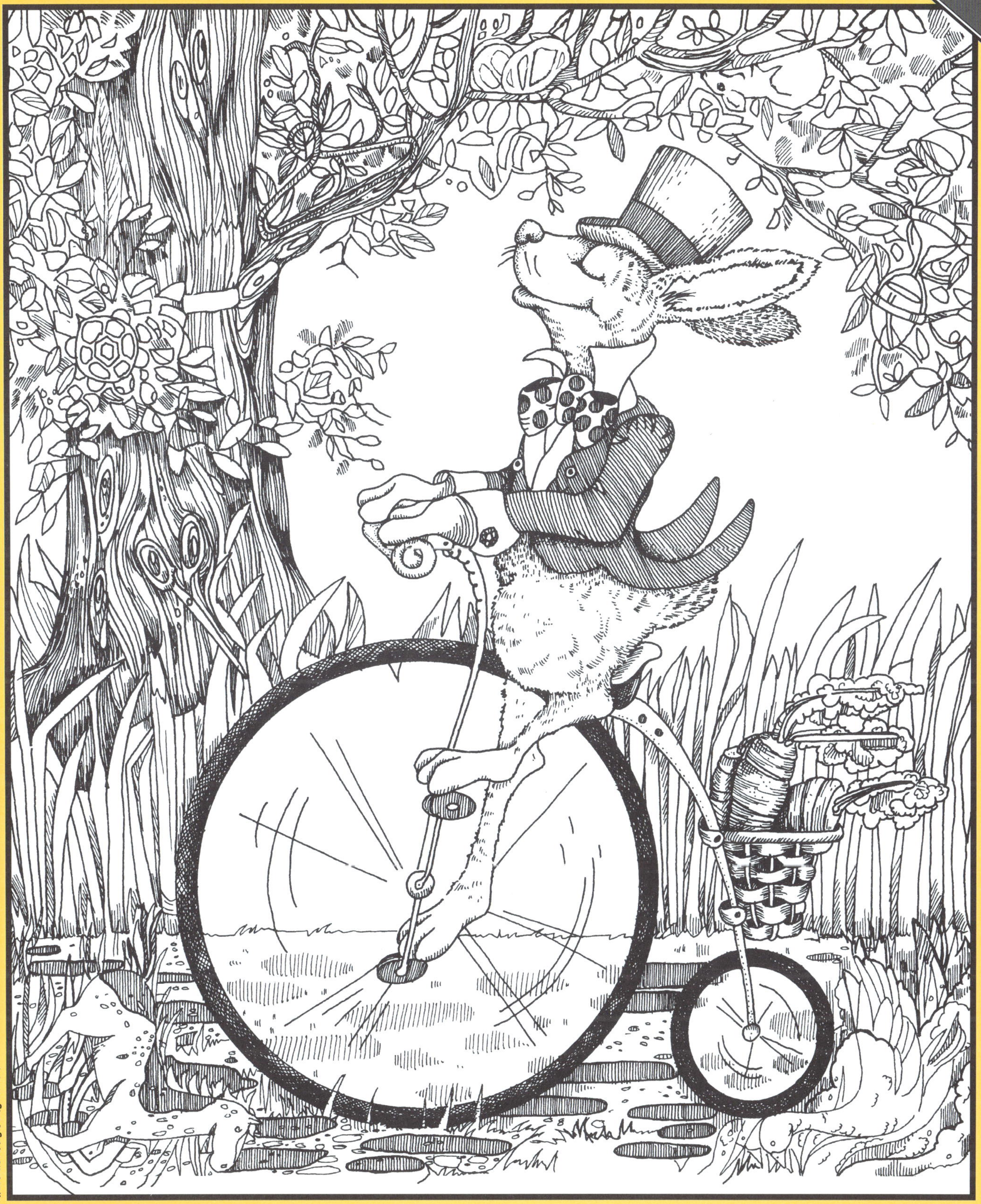

오스트레일리아 관광버스 Tour Bus Down Under

부메랑 boomerang, 바나나 두 개 2 bananas, 못 nail, 사과 apple, 양말 sock, 포크 fork, 앵무새 parrot, 벙어리장갑 mitten, 부채 fan, 생쥐 세 마리 3 mice, 연필 pencil, 숟가락 spoon

Illustrated by Valeri Gorbachev

요트 레이스 Yacht Race

박쥐 bat, 양초 candle, 유령 ghost, 남성 정장용 모자 top hat, 아이스크림콘 ice-cream cone, 막대 아이스크림 ice-cream bar, 벙어리장갑 mitten, 바늘 needle, 연필 pencil, 삼각기 pennant, 양말 sock, 뾰족 모자 pointy hat

Illustrated by Janet Robertson

105

다리 위에 멈춘 고장 난 차 Breakdown on the Bridge

신발 shoe, 종 bell, 벙어리장갑 mitten, 물고기 fish, 삽 shovel, 아이스크림콘 ice-cream cone, 연필 pencil, 크로케 나무망치 croquet mallet, 나사 screw, 치약 튜브 tube of toothpaste, 열쇠 key, 돋보기 magnifying glass

운하의 곤돌라들 Gondolas on the Canal

피자 조각 slice of pizza, v자형 뼈(위시본) wishbone, 손도끼 hatchet, 오리 duck, 상어 shark, 뾰족 모자 pointy hat, 신발 shoe, 크레용 crayon, 병 bottle, 칫솔 toothbrush, 털모자 knitted hat, 삼각기 pennant

Illustrated by Kit Wray

리프트 타고 정상으로 Lift to the Top

나비 butterfly, 체리 cherry, 초승달 crescent moon, 달걀 egg, 낚싯바늘 fishhook, 깃발 flag, 포크 fork, 국자 ladle, 막대사탕 lollipop, 펴놓은 책 open book, 연필 pencil, 상어 shark, 압정 tack, 찻잔 teacup, 테니스공 tennis ball, 벌레 worm

Illustrated by Arieh Zeldich

시험비행 Test Flight

손전등 flashlight, 빵 덩어리 loaf of bread, 망치 hammer, 새 bird, 쌍안경 binoculars, C 글자 letter C, 못 nail, 연 kite, 물 주전자 pitcher, 클라리넷 clarinet, 바이올린 활 violin bow, 고양이의 얼굴 cat's head, 하키 스틱 hockey stick, 모자 hat

Illustrated by Elizabeth Allyn Hendricks

109

누가 빨리 내려갈까 Race to the Bottom

사과 심 apple core, 그림 붓 artist's brush, 바나나 banana, 종 bell, 책 book, 나비 butterfly, 당근 carrot, 쓰레받기 dustpan, 손전등 flashlight, 꽃 flower, 골프채 golf club, 바늘 needle, 페인트 붓 paintbrush, 연필 pencil, 푸시핀 pushpin, 반지 ring, 삽 shovel, 빵 조각 slice of bread, 케이크 조각 slice of cake, 숟가락 spoon, 찻잔 teacup, 치약 튜브 tube of toothpaste, 꽃병 vase, 양초 candle

Illustrated by Charles Jordan

반가운 귀항 Return from the Sea

새 bird, 황새 stork, 캥거루 두 마리 2 kangaroos, 다리미 iron, 열쇠 key, 고양이 두 마리 2 cats, 종 bell, 기타 guitar, 토끼 rabbit, 찻잔 teacup, 양말 sock, 허리띠 belt, 바다 갈매기 seagull

Illustrated by Valeri Gorbachev

장거리 자전거 여행 Long-Distance Ride

안전핀 safety pin, 접은 우산 closed umbrella, 푸시핀 pushpin, 머그잔 mug, 양초 candle, 그림 붓 artist's brush, 부침용 주걱 spatula, 삽 shovel, 벙어리장갑 mitten, 깃털 feather, 못 nail, 연필 pencil

교외 드라이브
A Drive in the Country

어촌마을 Fisherman's Cove

호두 walnut, 물개 seal, 토끼 rabbit, 옥수수 ear of corn, 뾰족 모자 pointy hat, 병 jar, 염소의 얼굴 goat's head, 핸드백 purse, 개 dog, 토템기둥(원주민사회에서 토템을 그리거나 조각한) totem pole, 닻 anchor, 탁자 table, 연 kite, 포도 grapes, 물고기 fish

Illustrated by Jeri Simkus

자전거 탄 토끼 Bunny on a Bike

나비 butterfly, 케이크 조각 slice of cake, 양초 candle, 당근 carrot, 컵케이크 cupcake, 아이스크림콘 ice-cream cone, 음표 musical note, 연필 pencil, 푸시핀 pushpin, 드라이버 screwdriver, 숟가락 spoon, 압정 tack

뭉게구름 배경의 요트들 Ahead of the Clouds

샐러리 celery, 햄스터 hamster, 호두 walnut, 연필 pencil, 닻 anchor, 깃털 feather, 독수리의 얼굴 eagle's head, 돌고래 dolphin, 양말 sock, 망원경 telescope, 물고기 fish, 빵 조각 slice of bread, 해마 sea horse

미끄러운 비탈길 즐기기 Slippery Slope

장갑 glove, 하키 스틱 hockey stick, 백조 swan, 고양이 cat, 파이 pie, 숟가락 spoon, 핫도그 hot dog, 새 bird, 클로버 clover, 요정의 얼굴 elf's head, 백열전구 light bulb, 토끼 rabbit, 거북이 turtle, 양의 얼굴 lamb's head, 요정의 모자 elf's hat, 하트 heart

농약 살포 비행기 Crop Duster

사다리 ladder, 괭이 hoe, 골프채 golf club, 연 kite, 그림 붓 artist's brush, 갈퀴 rake, 아이스크림콘 ice-cream cone, 우표 stamp, 피자 조각 slice of pizza, 깃발 flag, 펴놓은 책 open book, 부츠 boot, 반지 ring, 뱀 snake, 파이 조각 slice of pie, 바늘 needle, 머핀 팬 muffin pan

Illustrated by Millard Hall

중장비 작업장 Heavy Equipment

120

자전거 공기 주입기 bicycle pump, 크레용 crayon, 눈삽 snow shovel, 포도 grapes, 드라이버 screwdriver, 깔때기 funnel, 서류가방 briefcase, 의자 chair, 올빼미 owl, 부츠 boot, 화분 flower pot, 사과 반쪽 apple half, 그림 붓 artist's brush, 생일 케이크 조각 slice of cake with a candle, 돋보기 magnifying glass, 막대 아이스크림 ice-cream bar, 옷걸이 coat hanger, 카누 canoe, 손전등 flashlight, 펴놓은 책 open book, 안전핀 safety pin, 파이 조각 slice of pie, 뾰족 모자 pointy hat, 전화기 telephone, 카우보이모자 cowboy hat, 꽃 flower, 잔(손잡이가 없고 굽이 달린) goblet

Illustrated by Charles Jordan

121

특별구매 Special Purchase

사다리 ladder, 잔(손잡이가 없고 굽이 달린) goblet, 칫솔 toothbrush, 종이비행기 paper airplane, 핸드벨 handbell, 책 book, 안경 eyeglasses, 빗자루 broom, 하트 heart, 도미노 패 domino, 편지봉투 envelope, 요요 yo-yo, 도끼 ax, 골프채 golf club, 부침용 주걱 spatula, 골프공 golf ball, 편자(말발굽에 붙이는 쇳조각) horseshoe, 반지 ring, 하키 스틱 hockey stick, 깃발 flag, 단추 button, 큐브 cube, 페인트 붓 paintbrush, 양초 candle, 거북이 turtle, 지팡이 모양 사탕 candy cane, 빗 comb, 부츠 boot, 유리컵 drinking glass, 신호기 pennant

즐거운 여행! Bon Voyage

초승달 crescent moon, 하트 heart, 핸드벨 handbell, 사다리 ladder, 부침용 주걱 spatula, 클립 paper clip, 편지봉투 envelope, 칫솔 toothbrush, 부츠 boot, 하키 스틱 hockey stick, 자석 magnet, 꽃삽 trowel, 부메랑 boomerang

Illustrated by Arieh Zeldich

비탈 아래로 프리라이딩 Freeriding Downhill

그림 붓 artist's brush, 빗 comb, 초승달 crescent moon, 왕관 crown, 찻잔 teacup, 아이스크림콘 ice-cream cone, 막대 아이스크림 ice-cream bar, 벙어리장갑 mitten, 못 nail, 양말 sock, 파이 조각 slice of pie, 칫솔 toothbrush, 치약 튜브 toothpaste

하늘을 수놓은 멋진 에어 쇼
Air Show

도전! 슈퍼 챌린지!
12개의 숨은그림을 찾아라!

통나무 나르기 Loads of Logs

골프채 golf club, 그림 붓 artist's brush, 깃털 feather, 막대 아이스크림 ice-cream bar, 연 kite, 펜 pen, 괭이 hoe, 삽 shovel, 파이 조각 slice of pie, 당근 carrot, 못 nail, 접은 우산 closed umbrella, 프라이팬 frying pan, 깔때기 funnel, 크레용 crayon, 케이크 조각 slice of cake, 안전핀 safety pin, 부침용 주걱 spatula, 머그잔 mug, 연필 pencil, 펜치 pliers, 양초 candle, 벙어리장갑 mitten, 숟가락 spoon, 푸시핀 pushpin, 반지 ring, 펴놓은 책 open book

Illustrated by Charles Jordan

금문교를 지나 Through the Golden Gate

물고기 fish, 망치 hammer, 쥐 mouse, 돌고래 dolphin, 머그잔 mug, 조개껍질 seashell, 포크 fork, 나비 butterfly, 연필 pencil, 깃털 feather, 바다 갈매기 seagull, 나뭇잎 leaf, 전원 콘센트 electrical outlet

Illustrated by Glen Dines

정답

▼4페이지

▼5페이지

▼6페이지

▼7페이지

▼8페이지

▼9페이지

▼10페이지

▼11페이지

▼12페이지

131

정답

▼13페이지

▼14페이지

▼15페이지

▼16-17페이지

▼18페이지

▼19페이지

▼20페이지

▼21페이지

정답

▼22페이지

▼23페이지

▼24페이지

▼25페이지

▼26-27페이지

▼28페이지

▼29페이지

▼30페이지

정답

▼31페이지

▼32-33페이지

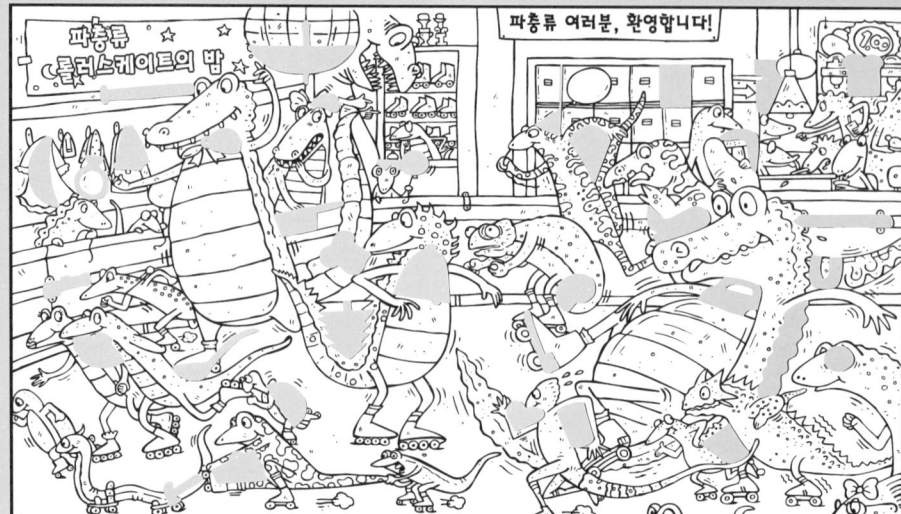

▼34페이지

▼35페이지

▼36-37페이지

▼38페이지

정답

▼39페이지

▼40페이지

▼41페이지

▼42페이지

▼43페이지

▼44-45페이지

▼46페이지

정답

▼47페이지

▼48-49페이지

▼50-51페이지

▼52페이지

▼53페이지

▼54-55페이지

정답

▼56페이지

▼57페이지

▼58페이지

▼59페이지

▼60페이지

▼61페이지

▼62페이지

▼63페이지

▼64페이지

정답

▼65페이지

▼66페이지

▼67페이지

▼68-69페이지

▼70페이지

▼71페이지

▼72페이지

▼73페이지

정답

▼74페이지

▼75페이지

▼76페이지

▼77페이지

▼78페이지

▼79페이지

▼80페이지

▼81페이지

▼82페이지

정답

▼83페이지

▼84-85페이지

▼86페이지

▼87페이지

▼88페이지

▼89페이지

▼90페이지

▼91페이지

정답

▼92-93페이지

▼94페이지

▼95페이지

▼96-97페이지

▼98페이지

▼99페이지

▼100페이지

정답

▼101페이지

▼102페이지

▼103페이지

▼104페이지

▼105페이지

▼106페이지

▼107페이지

▼108페이지

▼109페이지

정답

▼110 – 111페이지

▼112페이지

▼113페이지

▼114페이지

▼115페이지

▼116페이지

▼117페이지

▼118페이지

143

정답

▼119페이지

▼120-121페이지

▼122-123페이지

▼124페이지

▼125페이지

▼126-127페이지